Susie lived alone
in a neat little nest.
She was a very fine bird
with a bright pink crest.

One fine day,
Susie invited a guest—
and her bird-friend Stella
flew in from the West.

Stella wore sneakers
and a polka-dot vest.
She had curly green feathers
and a pretty blue crest.

3

Susie thought Stella
was simply the best.
She didn't know Stella
would be such a pest.

When Susie served salad
and worms to her guest,
Stella gobbled her snack
and then finished the rest!

When Susie and Stella
had a painting contest,
Stella splattered purple
all over the nest!

When Susie had to study
for an arithmetic test,
Stella decided
to tap dance with zest!

When Susie showed Stella
her costume chest,
Stella scattered clothing
north, east, south and west!

When Susie lay down
to take a short rest
Stella woke her right up
by braiding her crest!

"Stella," cried Susie,
"I have to protest!
You've brought nothing but trouble
into my nest!"

Stella the bird hid her beak in her vest.
"I'm so very sorry I was such a pest.
I just got so excited
'cause you are the best!"

Next Susie said,
"Stella, you aren't a pest.
You're a very fun friend—
I think YOU'RE the best!"

When the visit was over,
before Stella flew West,
she hugged her pal Susie.
She then hugged the nest!

Listen to the riddle sentences. Add the right letter or letters to the -est sound to finish each one.

1 A compass will help you to find north, south, east, and __est.

2 I like all animals, but I like birds the __est!

3 The little birds collected twigs to build themselves a __est.

4 When you visit someone's home you are a ___est.

5 I need to study my spelling words for tomorrow's big __est.

6 I can't finish my sandwich. Do you want the ___est?

7 When I bother my brother, he calls me a ___est.

8 A sweater without the sleeves is called a ___est.

9 It would be really neat to find a treasure ____est!

10 I bet you'll win first prize if you enter the _____est.

Now make up some new riddle sentences using - est

-est Cheer

Give a great holler, a cheer, a yell

For all of the words that we can spell

With an E, S, and T that make the sound –est,

You'll find it in nest and vest and best.

Three little letters, that's all that we need

To make a whole family of words to read!

Make a list of other –est words. Then use them in the cheer!